The Super-Bride's Guide For Dodging Wedding Pitfalls

Gloria Hander Lyons

Blue Sage Press

The Super-Bride's Guide for Dodging Wedding Pitfalls

Inquires should be addressed to:
Blue Sage Press
48 Borondo Pines
La Marque, TX 77568
www.BlueSagePress.com

ISBN-13: 978-0-9790618-4-4
ISBN-10: 0-9790618-4-9

Library of Congress Control Number: 2007902132

First Edition: April, 2007

Printed in the United States of America

Table of Contents

Introduction

The Super-Bride's Guide for Dodging Wedding Pitfalls

The good news is: you've found your perfect mate, you're head-over-heels in love, and you've decided to take the wedding commitment plunge. You've been dreaming all your life about this special day and how wonderful it will be. The bad news is: now you need to plan the big event.

It doesn't have to be all bad news, of course. Planning a wedding can be fun as long as you aren't overwhelmed by the details—and there are a lot of details involved.

But all you need is a little guidance to avoid some of the more common pitfalls of wedding planning. This book offers practical tips to help reduce stress during the planning process and keep your wedding on track.

It includes: a plan to get you organized, advice on setting and sticking to a budget, money-saving tips, helpful hints, and fun ideas to make your wedding unique.

It's a welcome relief for busy brides on a limited budget.

"I dreamed of a wedding of elaborate elegance, a church filled with family and friends. I asked him what kind of wedding he wished for. He said one that would make me his wife." Unknown

Pitfall #1: It's Got to Be Here Somewhere!

Coordinating all the details of a large event like a wedding can be exasperating. Not only are you spending a fairly large sum of money, you'll be making hundreds of decisions, managing numerous wedding vendors, mediating family disputes, dealing with your own emotional issues, and juggling all of the above with the added pressure of a looming deadline.

How do you keep track of all these details without loosing your sanity? The secret for planning any large event can be summed up in one word: ORGANIZATION.

The easiest way to organize all the parts of your wedding is to purchase a three-ring binder and add pocket dividers for each of the following categories that you might need:

- Guest List & Invitations
- Wedding Party
- Ceremony Site
- Reception Facility
- Wedding Attire
- Wedding Accessories
- Photographer/Videographer
- Baker
- Florist
- Caterer
- Musicians
- Transportation
- Honeymoon

As you make decisions and purchases for your wedding, place the details into the appropriate section of your wedding binder.

All information pertaining to your wedding should be kept in your binder, including receipts, contracts, names, addresses, phone numbers, fabric swatches, etc., so that you or those assisting you will know where to find it.

Keeping everything in one place will make your planning much less stressful. You'll have instant access to all your wedding information whenever a question arises—and it will.

Remember that organization is the key to keeping your wedding plans on track and keeping your stress level to a minimum. So be vigilant about adding all your receipts and contracts to your binder.

It will become your anchor in the storm as the wedding planning escalates toward the final event. Guard it with your life, because it truly can be a life saver!

Helpful Hints:

- If you are planning a fairly large wedding, don't try to do everything yourself. Delegate as many of the tasks as you can to willing family members or friends. And don't forget to ask your groom for help; he will be able to make a valuable contribution and feel less like an outsider. Planning your wedding should be fun—not exhausting. Try to enjoy the process with your groom and create fond memories that you can carry with you into your marriage.

- Be weather-wise when choosing the date for your wedding. Don't set the date during a snowy month if you live in a state that is prone to blizzards and avoid hurricane season if you're headed for a tropical island. Other weather-related issues to consider: rainy season, tornado season or unbearable heat waves if you live in an area where these conditions occur.

- Try not to become obsessed with making your event perfect. All brides dream of having the perfect wedding, but keep in mind that mistakes are going to happen and not everything will turn out the way you had hoped. Try to keep things in perspective and remember that the most important issue is the marriage—not the wedding.

- If you plan to change your last name and probably your address when you marry, there are dozens of institutions, companies and organizations you'll need to notify. Below is a list of a few to include on your list:

    - Driver's license
    - Social security card
    - Passport
    - Voter registration
    - Car registration
    - Insurance policies
    - Post office
    - Checking and savings accounts
    - Employer
    - Credit cards
    - Library card
    - Magazine subscriptions

Fun Ideas:

- Cover your wedding binder with attractive fabric or paper to make it more special and unique. It will also be easier to locate if it doesn't look like an ordinary binder.

- Cover a medium-size cardboard box that has a lift-off lid, or a hat box, with pretty fabric or paper to make a wedding memory box for saving invitations, dried flowers, photographs and other memorabilia from your wedding parties, bridal showers and wedding event.

- Keep a daily journal during the wedding planning process. Be sure to include your feelings, special moments, surprises, disappointments and humorous happenings. It will be fun to read years later. And even more special to share with your daughter or future daughter-in-law when they start to plan their own weddings.

Pitfall #2: You Spent What?

Yes, this is one of the most important events of your life and probably the biggest party you'll ever throw, but out-of-control spending can wreck this train before it leaves the station.

Before you start to shop, meet with those who are paying for the wedding, whether it is you and the groom, your parents, his parents or a combination of all three, and set a firm and realistic budget. Make a list of everything you'll need to purchase for your wedding. Decide which categories are most important to you and the groom and divide your funds accordingly.

Do you want an outrageously expensive dress? Do you want a fantastic band at your reception? Do you want 300 guests or just a few guests at a fabulous destination? Negotiate each category and assign a dollar amount for each one.

Financial rifts are the number one cause of discord between married couples. Don't start your life together on a really bad note. Agree on your budget before making any purchases. Keep it at the front of your binder for easy access and stick to it as closely as possible.

Helpful Hints:

- Set your wedding budget slightly smaller than you think you can actually afford. This will give you a margin for error in case one or two items turn out to be more expensive than you expected.

- If you and the groom are having trouble agreeing on your wedding priorities, it can help to write each important category, such as cake, photography, food, music or wedding dress on an index card. Spread the cards out on a table and move them around until you both agree on the order of importance. Transfer the list to a piece of paper and use it to plan your wedding budget.

- As you make the purchases from your wedding list, be sure to replace the estimated costs with the actual amount you paid for each item. Some items will cost more than you allotted and others might cost less. You'll need to adjust the figures accordingly as you shop, in order to stay within your budget.

- Don't automatically assume that just because you have a limited wedding budget you can't afford the services of a wedding consultant. Sometimes advice from an expert can save you money in the long run by helping you to avoid costly mistakes and recommending reputable vendors. You might consider hiring a wedding planner for limited planning assistance or just for the day of your wedding to help with the last minute "rush".

Pitfall #3: The Runaway Guest List

Setting a budget and prioritizing your funds will help determine the number of guests you can invite to the wedding. This is one area that can get out of hand quickly, especially when you're dealing with the emotional issues of family members.

This decision will be the first test of your partnership with your future husband to present a united front against all odds. It is, after all, your wedding, and the two of you need to set your budget priorities with regard to the number of guests you are willing to accommodate.

The more people you invite, the larger the reception facility and amount of food you will need, which means you will have less money to spend on the other categories for your wedding—such as cost of food per guest, entertainment, flowers, wedding attire, honeymoon, etc.

Only the bride and groom can decide what their priorities are for the number of guests to invite, because it will directly affect all the other budgetary decisions made for the wedding. Do you love the idea of being surrounded by hundreds of well-wishers or would you prefer to share your special day with just a few close friends and family members?

After you've agreed on the number of guests to invite, be sure to make a typed master list of all their names, including addresses and phone numbers, and keep it in your wedding binder. You will need to refer to this information numerous times during your wedding planning process.

Number each address on your list that will receive an invitation. For example, one through 50, or however many addresses (not guests) there are on the list. This will help you determine the number of invitations to order and the number of postage stamps you will need to purchase for mailing the invitations.

You can use your master guest list to record the R.S.V.P. responses from your guests. These responses will determine the amount of food and/or cake you will need to order for the wedding.

Also, allow a space on your guest list to record any gift received and when you mailed a thank you note.

Your master guest list is important information that you will need during the planning process for your wedding, so take care to create an accurate and legible document.

Helpful Hints:

- When sending response cards with your invitations, write the invitation number (the number that corresponds to the address on your guest list) on the back of the enclosed response card. If the guest forgets to fill in a name on the response card, you will know who sent it.

- Simplify the gift-giving process for your guests. Register at a couple of stores: one upscale department store for more expensive items like china and crystal, and a discount or home improvement store for less expensive, practical items like small appliances. Make sure the stores are accessible both locally and nationally for out of town guests.

Money Saving Tip:

- If you're looking for ways to cut wedding costs, the guest list is a good place to start. On a limited budget, you have basically two choices where the number of guests is concerned: having a modest wedding with a large crowd, or the wedding you really want with fewer guests. Of course you want to include your close friends and family, but do you really need to invite all of your parents' friends, associates and neighbors? Unless you have an unlimited wedding budget, trim the guest list down to the absolute "must-invites".

Fun Idea:

- Set up a wedding website for guests, as well as your wedding party, to keep everyone informed about the planning progress. Post photos of shopping trips, engagement parties, bridal showers, etc., complete with descriptive captions, to help your guests feel more involved and create anticipation for your event.

  You can also post maps, directions and hotel and local restaurant information for your out-of-town guests, to make their stay more enjoyable.

Pitfall #4: An Invitation to Disaster!

After deciding on your guest list and setting the date and location for your big event, you'll need to order invitations. They can be ordered from various card shops, print shops, office supply stores, catalogs or online using your computer.

Unless you are using a computer to print them yourself, the most important thing to remember when ordering your invitations is to allow extra time for them to arrive, in case there are any printing errors.

If the invitations are printed with the wrong date, time or location, not to mention the all important names of the participants, you'll need to reorder them.

Be sure to proof your invitations CAREFULLY as soon as they arrive. Sending out incorrect information to your wedding guests can spell disaster for your event.

Also factor into the ordering process the amount of time it will take you to address your invitations. This can vary widely, depending on how many invitations you'll be mailing and whether you are writing them out by hand or printing the addresses on the envelopes using a computer.

After proofing and addressing your invitations, mail them at least four weeks prior to the wedding—especially if you have a lot of guests coming in from out of town.

Another important detail to consider before dropping your invitations in the mailbox is correct postage. Not all invitations are created equal in the weight department. Some weigh more than one ounce; therefore, one first-class postage stamp will not suffice.

After assembling the invitations, complete with all enclosures, take one to the post office and have it weighed to determine the exact amount of postage required. This will ensure that your invitations aren't returned to you by the post office one week before your wedding. Talk about a disaster!

Keep all these factors in mind when ordering, addressing and mailing your invitations to ensure that your wedding stays on track.

Helpful Hints:

- Order about 10% more invitations than you think you'll need in case you have any last-minute additions to the guest list, and 25% more envelopes in case you make a mistake while addressing them.
- Don't forget to purchase thank you notes when ordering your invitations. Thank you notes should be sent PROMPTLY after receiving a bridal shower or wedding gift—preferably within two weeks.

Money Saving Tips:

- Be sure to consider postage costs when choosing your invitations. Some of the larger styles require more postage, which can add up fast when you're mailing 50 or more invitations.

- If you're crafty, make your own, one-of-a-kind invitations. See the suggestions on pages 17 through 20 for creative invitation ideas.

- Print your own invitations on a computer using blank card stock. You can find invitation kits at your local craft stores or office supply stores in a wide variety of styles to fit your wedding theme.

- Order post cards for response cards instead of envelopes and cards when you order your invitations. They will save on the invitation costs, as well as the postage costs.

- Include an R.S.V.P. phone number on the invitation instead of sending response cards. But you'll need to be vigilant about recording the responses on your master guest list since you won't have the written responses to confirm the number of guests later.

- Ask guests to respond on your personal wedding website instead of sending response cards.

- One of the newest trends in event invitations that would be perfectly acceptable for casual weddings is the e-mail invitation. You can create colorful invitations yourself using clip art or photos or use a website that offers this service, like e-vite.com.

Fun Idea:

- Theme weddings are fun and can make your event planning a lot easier. Just pick a theme, such as Victorian, Winter Wonderland, Mardi Gras, Western, Tropical Paradise, or any other theme that appeals to you, then make a list of every item, food, color, costume, activity or fact that fits into your theme idea.

  You might need to do some research for historical periods or foreign countries, but it will make your theme more authentic. The things you select from your list will be your guide for choosing the invitations, colors, decorations, flowers, food and favors for your wedding.

Creative Ideas for Invitations

When making your own invitations, get creative. They don't have to be flat pieces of paper. They can be three-dimensional objects, which are mailed or hand-delivered. Consider some of the following suggestions:

- For a beach theme wedding, purchase small, clear glass or plastic bottles with corks from a craft store (also available online). Print your wedding information on a piece of parchment paper, roll it up and tuck it inside the bottle. Add a bit of sand to the bottle before sealing it with a cork. Mail in a tissue lined box.

- Another idea for a beach theme wedding, with just a few guests, is to write your information on a small, inflated beach ball, using a permanent black marker. Mail in a tissue lined box or hand deliver.

- Purchase four-inch Styrofoam balls from your local craft store. Spray paint them black and attach a short length of rattan or plastic chain (also painted black) to make a "ball and chain". Print your wedding information on a card and attach it to the end of the chain. Mail the whole thing in a box lined with colorful tissue paper.

- For a Christmas theme wedding, print your information on Christmas stationery and tuck inside a small, inexpensive Christmas stocking. If you plan ahead, you can pick these up after Christmas for less than half price. Mail in a padded mailer.

- For a 1950's rock and roll theme, print your information onto colored card stock paper, cut out in circle shapes, sized to fit the center of old 45 rpm records and glue in place, using a glue stick or spray adhesive. Mail in a padded mailer.

- Send a video invitation. You and the groom can create a fun video recording of the two of you extending a personal invitation for your guests to join you at your special event. Copy the recording onto DVD's and make colorful labels that include your names and the date, place and time of your event. Attach a label to each DVD. Mail in a padded mailer.

- Everyone loves the gift of food. Place a few small pieces of divinity candy in a clear cellophane bag. Attach your invitation, which begins, "Love is Divine!" Mail in a pretty box that is lined with tissue paper.

- If the weather isn't too warm, you can mail your guests chocolate candy bars with a custom designed label. Use your computer to print your wedding invitations on colorful paper sized to fit the candy bar you plan to mail. Remove the original paper candy wrapper (leave the inner foil wrapper in place) and replace it with your invitation. Mail in a box lined with colorful tissue paper.

- For a really festive invitation, print the wedding information onto a small piece of paper, about 4" X 6", using your computer. Roll up into a tight scroll and place inside a large latex balloon. Use a small funnel to add a bit of colorful confetti. Inflate the balloon with helium and attach a 3-foot length of narrow ribbon. Hand deliver the invitations.

- If your wedding theme is hearts, purchase small heart boxes for your invitations. Using your computer, print the wedding information onto paper sized to fit inside the bottom of the heart box. Trace around the bottom of one of the boxes onto a piece of cardboard that is about 2" larger than the box. Cut out the heart, leaving a heart-shaped hole in the center of the cardboard piece. Use the piece of cardboard as a template to trace hearts onto your invitations. Cut them out and glue inside the bottom of each box, using a glue stick. Replace the lids on the boxes and tie a bow around each box using wide ribbon. Mail the heart boxes in a separate box or hand deliver them to your guests.

- Send your invitation inside a festive party cracker. Cut a 5" square of poster board, roll it into a tube, overlapping the ends 1/4" and tape together). Wrap it with colorful wrapping paper with the ends extending at least 3" beyond the tube on each end. Gather the wrapping paper close to one end of the tube and tie with ribbon to secure. Print your wedding information on a piece of colorful paper sized to fit the cracker, roll it up and tuck it inside. Add a few individually wrapped pieces of candy then gather the wrapping paper at the open end and tie with ribbon. Mail in a box or hand deliver.

- Give your guests a puzzle to solve in order to reveal the information on your invitation. Create a simple photo puzzle with your invitation on the back. Copy a photo of you and the groom (black and white or color), about 5" X 7". Glue it to the same size piece of sturdy cardboard, like tag board, using a glue stick or spray adhesive. Print your invitation using your computer and glue to the back of the cardboard. Cut the puzzle into about six or eight pieces—you don't want your guests to have to work too hard to solve the puzzle. Mail the puzzle pieces in a padded envelope.

- For a tropical paradise theme, tuck your information inside a large sea shell and mail in a box lined with colorful tissue paper.

- A really fun option for a tropical paradise theme is to purchase plastic pink flamingoes from your local party store. Print your wedding information on a card and tie it around the bird's neck. You and your groom can make a late-night, clandestine run to plant the birds in your guests' yards. Your invitation is not only fun to deliver, but a surprise for your guests.

Pitfall #5: A Cast of Thousands

The wedding party is another area that can get out of control quickly and erode your wedding dollars in a hurry. Once again, you and the groom will need to prioritize this category to keep it in perspective with the overall vision you have for your wedding.

Before you round up all your friends and bestow the honorary title of bridesmaid on each one, take stock of the ceremony site you are considering. How many attendants can you actually accommodate comfortably at the facility?

Also, budget-wise, the number of attendants directly affects the number of wedding guests, size of the ceremony site and reception site facilities needed, and flowers and food required. This is definitely an area that you and the groom will need to agree on in advance while setting your wedding budget.

Decide how large you want your wedding to be before you start choosing your attendants. Keep in mind that a giant wedding party is not suitable for an informal wedding. If you really do want a cast of thousands, then choose an appropriate facility and level of formality.

After agreeing on the number of attendants and choosing the wedding party members, keep a list of the name, address and phone numbers of each person who will be in your wedding party, including parents, grandparents, groomsmen, bridesmaids, ushers, etc. These days, it's also helpful to have each person's e-mail address. It can make contacting them much easier and quicker.

Beside each wedding party member's name, list that person's role in your wedding. This information will be helpful in contacting the various members during the planning stages of your wedding, especially if you have someone assisting you who might not know the other members.

Your list will also make it easier for you to order flowers. Your florist will have the exact number of participants and know which type of floral arrangement to order for each one (boutonniere, corsage, bouquet, basket, etc.).

This list will come in handy again when it's time to purchase wedding party gifts.

Be sure to take your wedding party list with you to the wedding rehearsal, ceremony and reception. It will be invaluable when distributing flowers and lining up the wedding party for the ceremony and group photographs.

Helpful Hints:

- If you are planning to have a ring bearer and/or flower girl, it is recommended that they be at least four years old. Even at that age, you should be prepared to expect the unexpected.

- It's best to place (actually, sew) fake wedding rings on the ring bearer's pillow and give the real ones to the maid of honor and best man.

- If your bridesmaids don't know each other, it's a good idea to gather them all together for lunch or dinner sometime before the wedding, so they'll have a chance to meet before the big day.

Money-Saving Idea:

- As with the guest list, keeping your wedding attendants to a minimum will help keep your wedding budget in check. Unless you have unlimited wedding funds, trim the attendant list to the absolute "must haves".

Fun Ideas:

- Make your wedding day really special. Ask your mother or grandmother to be your matron of honor. It's a thoughtful gesture that she will cherish forever.

- Need a few new ideas for gifts for your wedding attendants? Try some of the following:

    - A gift certificate to their favorite restaurant
    - Tickets to a sporting event, play or concert
    - A gift certificate for a manicure or carwash
    - Movie tickets
    - Souvenirs from your honeymoon location

- Set up a wedding website to keep your wedding party, friends and family up to date as your wedding plans progress. Having a website also makes it easier to let everyone know about upcoming appointments (such as dress or tuxedo fittings) and events.

- Plan a relaxing weekend with your girlfriends instead of a one-night bachelorette party. Camp out at the beach, rent a mountainside cabin or pamper yourselves at a spa retreat. It's a great way to de-stress before the big day arrives.

Pitfall #6: Get Me to the Church On Time

If you plan to hold your ceremony at a church, you'll need to select the location and the clergy who will perform the ceremony. If you'll be using the church where you normally attend services, this facility will determine the size of wedding you can plan, including the number of attendants you choose and the number of wedding guests you can invite.

Keep this factor in mind before making your final decision about your ceremony site. Will the facility accommodate the overall vision you have for your wedding? If not you'll need to choose a different location.

Find out about any fees or rules that might affect your decision to use the facility. Make sure you understand and agree to any restrictions the church imposes, such as photography, videotaping, music, decorations, wedding attire, etc., before reserving the site. You don't want any last-minute surprises that could spoil your plans.

Get the name and phone number of the contact person at the church in case you have questions later. You'll also need this information to schedule your wedding rehearsal and arrange for decorating the facility on the day of your wedding.

Find out if there is a wedding coordinator at the church who will be present to assist with the rehearsal and wedding. Many churches offer this service. If not, you might consider hiring a wedding consultant to handle this part of your wedding, or ask a friend or family member to take on the task.

Meet with the clergy to discuss the wording of your vows. This is a life-time commitment you're making in front of witnesses, so you don't want any surprises at the altar. If you and the groom plan to write your own vows, be sure to confirm your decision with the person who will be officiating at your ceremony.

Also, discuss any special events you might want to include during the ceremony, such as lighting a unity candle, having a vocalist perform or reading a special poem.

Choose the date and time for your ceremony and wedding rehearsal. Get all of this information in writing and keep it in your wedding binder.

Helpful Hints:

- Before ordering your invitations, call to confirm the date and time of your ceremony. Mistakes can happen, and you might need to choose a new date for your event.

- If you plan to use unity candles during your wedding ceremony, be sure to light them once before the wedding to break them in. Many nervous brides and grooms have had trouble lighting candles that were brand new.

Money Saving Idea:

- To save on decorating costs and transportation hassles, have the ceremony at the same location as the reception or vice versa.

Fun Ideas:

- Instead of turning your backs to your guests during the ceremony, why not face them as you exchange your vows, or try seating guests in a circle instead of traditional rows.

- Instead of having your father escort you down the aisle, leaving your mother sitting on the pew, why not give both parents the honor?

- Why not have the groom and groomsmen walk down the aisle before the bridesmaids, instead of sneaking in from a side door? Don't they deserve to be in the spotlight, as well? And, as mentioned above, let the groom's parents escort him down the aisle.

- You and the groom can write your own, unique wedding vows. There are hundreds of examples to browse through online. Discussing some of the issues you discover in your research can be an important eye-opener. Also, writing your own vows makes them much more meaningful (and specific if there's something extra you want to include) than repeating someone else's words.

- Following an old Irish custom, ring a small hand bell after you recite your vows. Keep the bell to remind you of the promises you made to each other, and start a new tradition of ringing the bell on your anniversary.

- Ask your parents to renew their vows or invite all of your married guests to reaffirm their love during the ceremony. It will be a memorable occasion for everyone.

- Have both sets of parents light a unity candle during the ceremony to signify the merging of your two families.

Pitfall #7: Where's the Party?

After the ceremony is over, the celebrating begins. The reception is, after all, just a big party for friends and family to congratulate the newly married couple.

The choices for wedding receptions range widely from the simple cake-and-punch affair held in the church reception hall to a formal sit-down dinner at a fancy hotel.

Again, that nasty budget rears its ugly head. But if you and the groom have set your priorities ahead of time, then the reception you have planned will be a perfect fit.

Choosing the Reception Facility:

To help avoid pitfalls at the reception, get the facts about any facility you are considering. Whether you are choosing an all-inclusive banquet facility or stand-alone meeting hall, be sure to get the following information:

- Make sure the site you choose is large enough to accommodate comfortably the number of guests you plan to invite. Does it have ample parking and restroom facilities for your guests?

- If you plan to have dancing at your reception, make sure there is enough space for dancing, appropriate flooring for a dance floor and sufficient electrical requirements for a band or DJ.

- Find out what the restrictions are regarding the use of birdseed or wedding bubbles if you want your guests to be able to send you and the groom off in style at the end of the reception.

- What is the facility's policy regarding decorations? Can you hang decorations from the ceiling or on the walls? What about the use of candles?

- What is the facility's refund policy in case the wedding plans need to be changed or cancelled?

Stand-Alone Banquet Facilities:

If you choose to hold your reception at an all-inclusive banquet facility or hotel ballroom, pretty much everything is included from food to servers. But if you decide to reserve a stand-alone meeting hall for your reception, you are responsible for providing everything yourself. For this type of facility, be sure to get the following information:

- Make sure the kitchen is adequate to accommodate your caterer's needs, or your needs, if you are providing the food.

- Check to see if the facility can provide sufficient tables and chairs for your guests. If so, is there an extra charge for this service?

- What is their policy regarding alcohol on the premises? Most facilities charge an extra deposit and require that you hire a security guard when alcohol is being served.

- Will someone from the facility staff be on hand to deal with problems or questions, such as air conditioning or lighting?

- Who is responsible for clean-up after the event?

Choosing the Food:

Your wedding budget will determine what type of food you will serve at your reception. It might be just a cake and punch affair or a full-blown sit-down dinner. If you're not providing the food yourself, you'll need to choose a caterer.

When deciding on the food for your event, whether you are using the hotel caterer or hiring your own caterer for a reception at a meeting hall, ask to sample the food they will prepare. You don't want to pay a lot of money to feed your guests, only to be disappointed during the reception. As with all the wedding vendors you choose, check their references carefully.

Your master guest list will help determine the amount of food you'll need to order for your reception. All the details for number of guests, what food will be served and price per person should be included on your contract, as well as any extra fees such as set up charges, gratuities, cake cutting fees, etc. Make sure you understand the caterer's policies for deposits, payment schedule and cancellation.

After you have chosen the facility for your reception and possibly a caterer for your event, keep the vendors' names, phone numbers and your contracts and receipts in your wedding binder for easy access should a question or problem arise.

Helpful Hints:

- When giving the caterer your final head-count, don't forget to include meals for your DJ or band members, photographer and/or videographer and wedding consultant. Some caterers give discounts on vendor meals as a professional courtesy.

- Be sure to count the number of children's meals separately from the adults. Caterers usually charge less for children under 12 years old.

- Since you and the groom might not have a chance to eat much during the reception, have someone pack a small basket with leftover food and place it in your car to eat on your way to the airport or honeymoon hotel.

Money Saving Tips:

- Plan to have your wedding during an off-season month (November through April) to save money and get better access to the more popular wedding vendors and sites.

- Set your wedding date on Friday or Sunday instead of Saturday. You'll have more choices for facilities and vendors, and the prices are usually lower.

- Some facilities will provide the wedding cake or a champagne toast as part of a package deal, which can save you money over buying these items separately.

- Schedule your wedding in the afternoon (after lunch and before dinner) to avoid having to serve a full meal for your guests. Serve just cake or cake and light hors d'oeuvres.

- If serving alcohol would be a budget buster and you don't feel comfortable with a cash bar, offer your guests a champagne toast instead.

- Another option for serving alcohol on a budget is to rent a frozen drink machine and have a couple of friends make and serve Margaritas or Daiquiri's if these drinks will fit your wedding theme.

- For extra savings on food, ask friends or family members to bring hors d'oeuvres to be served at the reception, or have a potluck dinner. Be sure to put someone else in charge of keeping track of who's bringing what and setting up the food on your wedding day—you'll have enough to worry about.

- Take advantage of facilities that might be decorated for holidays, such as Christmas, to save on decorating costs.

Fun Ideas:

- Consider having your wedding and reception on a yacht or Mississippi-style paddle wheel boat. Other possibilities are: a historical site, such as a Victorian mansion, or museum or arboretum, such as an indoor rain forest or butterfly garden.

- Have a dessert reception instead of an expensive sit-down dinner or buffet. Be sure to write on the invitation, "Dessert reception to follow ceremony," so guests will know to eat dinner before the wedding.

  This type of reception is usually held in the late evening and includes every kind of sweet imaginable. Make the desserts eye appealing and delectable, such as fruit tarts, chocolate dipped strawberries, pretty pastries and chocolate fountains.

Pitfall #8: A Word About The Great Outdoors

If you've always dreamed of having your ceremony and reception in a beautiful garden or on a gorgeous hilltop, I have just two words for you: BACKUP PLAN. Outdoor weddings can be dreamy, but sometimes Mother Nature has other ideas.

In the weather category there is, of course, the unexpected rain shower—not to mention the occasional hail or wind storm. Then there is the unpredictable temperature. During what normally should be a comfortable time of year, the temperature can suddenly soar to 100 degrees or drop to a chilly 40. Did I mention bugs—ants, mosquitoes, bees and gnats, just to name a few?

I don't want to "rain" on your parade, because an outdoor wedding can be a beautiful event. Just be prepared to move indoors in case the unexpected becomes a reality.

That means you'll need a backup plan: move inside the house if you're in your own backyard, move to a pavilion if you're in a park, or at the very least, have a sturdy tent close by.

Helpful Hints:

- Consider having just your ceremony outside and the reception inside. That way, you'll have a back-up location for the ceremony if the weather doesn't cooperate.

- If you're planning to exchange vows at sunset during an outdoor ceremony, check out The Old Farmer's Almanac for the exact time the sun will make its glorious descent. You can also find the information online at almanac.com.

- At a sunset ceremony, make sure your guests aren't blinded by the glare. Don't face the guests' chairs toward the setting sun.

- Outdoor sites can sometimes be noisy with the sounds of wind, surf, etc. Consider renting clip-on microphones for yourself, your groom and the wedding officiant so your guests will be able to hear the ceremony.

- Plan for a windy day. Be sure to let your hair stylist know that your wedding will be outdoors so she can design a style that won't leave you looking frightful in your wedding photos.

- Also keep the wind factor in mind when choosing the style and fabrics for your wedding dress and those of your bridesmaids. You don't want your gown blowing up over your head during the ceremony.

- Incorporate citronella candles into your decorations at an outdoor wedding to help ward off insects. They will do double duty, casting a warm glow of light throughout the décor, as well as protecting your guests from annoying pests.

- For your wedding flowers, choose roses, orchids, or other hardy blooms that can stand up under the heat if your wedding is planned for summer. Warm temperatures can cause more fragile flowers to wilt.

- Don't order buttercream frosting on your wedding cake if your reception is being held outdoors and the weather is warm. The icing will melt and slide right off the cake!

- Make sure the caterer you choose to provide the food for your reception has experience preparing and serving food for outdoor events. They will also need to consider the temperature and wind factors when planning food choices and serving options.

- If your ceremony will take place outside in warm weather, be sure to keep this in mind when choosing the fabric and style of your dress, as well as your bridesmaids' dresses. Stick with strapless, sleeveless or short sleeved gowns, and lightweight, breathable fabrics.

- If the weather is warm, don't forget to provide cool drinks, like lemonade, ice water or punch for your guests to drink while they are waiting for the ceremony to begin.

Fun Ideas:

- Consider using an arch or trellis as the focal point for the ceremony that will frame you and the groom as you say your vows.

- If you're getting married during one of the warmer summer months, have your wedding programs printed on paddle-style fans. They'll do double duty, keeping your guests informed about the ceremony details, while keeping them cool during the event.

- If your ceremony and reception will continue into the night, use strings of lights or lanterns in the trees, candles on the tables, and luminarias on the ground to light pathways.

- If you're having a casual wedding on the beach or a tropical island theme in the backyard, add to the ambiance while keeping the drinks simple and inexpensive. Use a small row-boat or dinghy filled with ice and soft drinks, beer and wine coolers.

Pitfall #9: What's a Girl To Wear?

A common area of contention between wedding couples when the budget is fairly limited is how much to spend on the wedding dress. The bride, of course, wants to look and feel like a princess on her special day, which usually means a fair amount of the wedding budget will be allocated to her dress.

The groom, on the other hand, might feel that the money would be better spent on the wedding reception entertainment or honeymoon. To avoid starting off your marriage on the wrong foot, agree on a budget for all the wedding attire before the shopping begins.

Wedding attire includes your wedding gown, veil, and shoes; the bridesmaids' dresses and shoes; and the tuxedos and shoes for the men in the wedding party.

Will you be paying for the bridesmaids' dresses and groomsmen's tuxedo rentals or will the members of the wedding party pay for their own attire? These issues must be decided during the budget planning stage.

The wedding attire can range widely in price, and therefore can have a significant impact on your budget, so allocate a specific dollar amount for each category. Try to stick to your budget as closely as possible when making each choice for wedding attire.

Wedding Gown Shopping Tips

When shopping for your wedding gown, avoid going to too many shops in one day—it can be overwhelming.

It's a good idea to collect pictures of wedding gowns that appeal to you before you go dress shopping. But, even if you think you know the exact style of dress you want, be open to other styles.

What looks good in a picture might not work for you when you try it on. Also, the one you had in mind might not be the most flattering style for you. The bridal consultant at each shop can suggest styles that are suitable for your size and figure type.

Decide ahead of time what you want and need in a wedding gown, especially any of your physical features that you want to disguise or highlight. Also, keep in mind the level of formality for your wedding. Don't fall in love with an over-the-top formal gown when your wedding will be a casual afternoon affair.

Wear a strapless bra when shopping if you're considering a gown in that style and wear shoes with the same height of heel that you plan to wear on your wedding day.

Take someone along as a shopping companion whose opinion you trust. This might be your mother, your sister or your best friend, but don't take more than one person with you when shopping for your dress; too many opinions can be counterproductive.

Do take a camera with you in case you can't decide which dress you like best while shopping. Have someone take a picture of you wearing each dress you're considering, so you can study them at home later. Choosing the right dress can be frustrating, so take your time and don't rush into a decision you'll regret later.

A Word About Special Orders

Be careful when special ordering a dress. You'll be required to pay a NON-REFUNDABLE deposit of one third to one half the cost of the dress. Make sure it's the one you want because, if you change your mind, you can't get your deposit money back!

The sales contract for your order should include the size and color of the gown you're ordering, the manufacturer's name, the style number, and a description of the gown (not just a store code). Make sure all your bases are covered because mistakes can happen.

Your wedding date and last acceptable date for delivery of the gown should also be included on the contract. Be sure to allow time for portraits and/or alterations in the last acceptable date.

Read the "fine print" at the bottom of the contract carefully and ask questions if you don't understand something. It's best to use a credit card to pay for your gown. You can protest the charges later if you don't receive the dress you ordered in acceptable condition or on time.

Dressing the "Maids"

In addition to choosing your own gown, you'll need to select dresses for your bridesmaids.

Try to pick a style and color that will be flattering and comfortable for a variety of shapes and sizes.

One dress silhouette that looks good on just about everyone is the A-line.

After choosing your bridesmaids' dresses, keep swatches of the dress fabric in the pocket folder of your wedding binder. They will come in handy when ordering the flowers for your wedding and shoes for your bridesmaids if you plan to have them dyed to match their dresses.

Place all the receipts and contracts for the wedding attire you purchase in your wedding binder in case a question arises later.

You'll need to keep track of any deposits and partial payments made on your dress, as well as alteration appointments and charges. These contracts and receipts are critical—you don't want the bridal shop holding your dress hostage on your wedding day because of a mix-up regarding payments.

Helpful Hints:

- Be sure you can move comfortably in the wedding dress you choose, especially if you plan to dance at your reception.
- Buy comfortable wedding shoes because you'll be on your feet most of the time that day, whether you're dancing or not.
- If your bridesmaids are a wide range of shapes and sizes, you might consider choosing the color and fabric of their dresses, and then let each maid choose her own dress style, so each one can look and feel her best.
- If you have a very short time to plan your wedding, pick a color (black is easy) and ask your bridesmaids to wear a dress of their choice in that color. You'll save yourself and your bridesmaids a lot of stress, not to mention money, for rush orders at bridal salons.

- Remind the groom and groomsmen to try on their tuxedos before leaving the tuxedo store when they pick them up. Mistakes can happen—you don't want to find out about them an hour before the wedding!

Money Saving Tips:

- Make your own wedding dress if you or a family member can sew. This is not only a good way to add your own personal touch to your wedding, but you'll have a one-of-a-kind dress.

- Hire a seamstress to make your wedding gown. But make sure she has experience sewing bridal fabrics, check for references and ask to examine samples of her previous work.

- Buy a white bridesmaid's dress or formal instead of a wedding gown. They are much less expensive, and can be just as beautiful, especially for a less formal, afternoon wedding.

- Shop at sample sales, where bridal stores mark down last season's wedding dresses to make room for new inventory.

- Buy your dress at a formal resale store; just be sure to check it carefully for stains or tears. Then consider selling it again at the same store after the wedding.

- Wear your mother's (or grandmother's) wedding dress if it can be altered to fit you. She will be thrilled to see her dress on you, and you'll save lots of money.

- Ask about alteration costs for any dress you are considering. Certain dress styles are more expensive to alter than others. These charges could put you over the top budget-wise.

- Make your own veil. Headpieces and tulle are available at most craft and fabric stores, along with books and patterns to show you how. This is another way to add a unique touch to your wedding.

- Borrow a headpiece or veil from a relative or friend. Not only will you be saving money, you'll be honoring the "something borrowed" tradition at the same time.

- Many bridal stores will offer a discount on wedding attire, including shoes and jewelry, if you buy your wedding gown AND the bridesmaids′ dresses there. Be sure to compare prices to make sure the discount is actually saving you money over buying the bridesmaids dresses elsewhere.

- Some tuxedo rental stores will supply the groom's tuxedo for free if you rent several tuxedos. It pays to do a bit of comparison shopping in this department.

Fun Ideas:

- Have a piece of your mother's wedding dress sewn into your gown in honor of the "something old" tradition.

- Instead of a traditional tiara headpiece, use sparkly accessories, such as a strand of crystals, pearls, or jeweled hairpins to dress up your hair.

- Wear a floral wreath for your headpiece (with or without a veil). Your bridesmaids can wear floral wreath headpieces, as well. If you, a friend or family member are crafty, you can make your own wreaths from either real or silk flowers.

- Add a splash of color to an all-white wedding dress with a colored sash tied around your waist that coordinates with the colors of your wedding theme.

- Get wild and crazy with your wedding dress! There's no law that says you have to wear white. Pastels can be beautiful for spring and summer weddings. In some cultures around the world, it's considered lucky for the bride to wear red. Go for it!

Pitfall #10: Let Them Eat Cake!

A baker usually provides the wedding cake for your wedding reception. Choose this person wisely! Whether you bestow the honor on your Great Aunt Lizzie or the most posh bakery in town, make sure your baker has considerable experience in the wedding cake department.

Your wedding cake is the focal point of the reception. It not only needs to look good and taste good, but it needs to stay together in one piece until you're ready to cut it.

The classical tiered wedding cake requires architectural expertise and not all bakers are up for the challenge. Check references and ask friends for referrals to make sure you are getting a baker with a good track record.

Allow plenty of time to shop around for your cake. Many couples make the mistake of leaving the cake to the last minute and are disappointed with the result.

Be sure to sample the cakes from several different bakeries before making your final choice. You don't want a cake that looks beautiful, but tastes like cardboard. Wedding cakes are expensive, so make sure you choose one that will make your wedding day memorable.

Your master guest list will help you determine the size of the cake and number of servings you will need to order. Get all details in writing for style of cake, size, flavor, decorations, cost per serving and delivery and set up charges. Also make sure you understand the baker's deposit and payment schedule, as well as cancellation policy.

Be sure to keep your baker's name and phone number in your wedding binder, as well as your contract, in case there are any last-minute problems.

Helpful Hints:

- Don't order buttercream frosting on your wedding cake if your reception is being held outdoors and the weather is warm. The icing will melt and slide right off the cake!

- Rolled fondant icing on a wedding cake is beautiful, but it doesn't actually taste as good as it looks. It is very sweet and a bit chewy; many people don't like the taste. If you really love the look, try it before you buy it.

Money Saving Tips:

- If you're having a very small wedding, but want a tiered wedding cake, ask the baker to add a fake layer at the base of your cake. You get a more impressive looking cake without the expense of more cake than you need.

- If you are having a very large wedding, order a cake smaller than you need in order to save money on the decorating costs. Have the baker make sheet cakes, which can be cut in the kitchen and brought to the serving table.

- Use fresh flowers to decorate your cake instead of paying for elaborate icing decorations. (Make sure they are pesticide-free. Most flowers from florists are not.)

- If you are lucky enough to have a friend or family member who has the expertise to bake a wedding cake to your satisfaction, then, by all means, go for it!

Fun Ideas:

- If you're having a theme wedding, be sure to continue it in your cake design. Whether it's Mardi Gras masks or pink flamingoes, your baker can use colored frosting and other decorations to create a cake to fit your wedding theme.

- Bake small, two-tiered wedding cakes for each of your guest tables instead of one large wedding cake. They will do double duty as centerpieces.

- Let the groom choose a cake that is shaped to represent his favorite hobby: perhaps a football if he's an avid football fan or a sailboat for a weekend sailor.

- Fun alternatives to a traditional wedding cake, that are also less expensive, are cupcakes, iced sugar cookies, doughnuts, or miniature pies or cheese cakes that are decorated and stacked on tiered serving platters.

- Decorate cupcakes and stack them on tiered serving plates for the centerpieces on your guest tables instead of having one big wedding cake. Make all the cupcakes ahead of time and freeze them. Decorate the day before the wedding to match your theme.

Pitfall #11: Tiptoe Through the Tulips

Most brides feel the second most important consideration for a wedding, after the dress, is flowers. Beautiful flowers definitely add to the ambiance of the wedding, but they can be pricey.

Be sure to compare services and prices of several florists before making your final decision. Make sure the florist is familiar with your ceremony and reception site locations. Also make sure they are aware of any rules or restrictions that might apply to decorations, such as pew bows or candelabras.

You don't want your florist dropping off the flowers at the wrong church and you don't want to pay for candelabras if your ceremony site doesn't allow them.

If possible, take your fabric swatches and photos of your wedding gown and bridesmaids dresses with you when ordering your flowers, so the florist can design bouquets that will be appropriate in size, style and color.

Take your wedding party list with you, also, to help determine the correct number of bouquets, corsages and boutonnieres you need to order.

Get all the details for your order in writing, including number and type of floral arrangements and color and type of flowers. Keep your contract and receipt in your binder and have it handy when the flowers are delivered to your wedding and reception sites in case there are any discrepancies.

Helpful Hints:

- Flowers such as lilies can leave a bright yellow stain on your wedding dress. Make sure your florist removes the stamens that can cause the stains.
- Choose roses, orchids, or other hardy blooms that can stand up under the heat if you're planning an outdoor wedding during the summer. Warm temperatures can cause more fragile flowers to wilt.
- If your florist will be dropping off your flowers on the wedding day instead of handing them out to each member of the wedding party, designate an assistant to receive the flowers and check your contract to make sure that the florist has delivered the correct type and number of flowers. Don't let that delivery person out of sight until you have determined that all the flowers are present and accounted for.

Money Saving Tips:

- Choose flowers that are in season, as well as ones that are not price-inflated because of a holiday, such as roses on Valentine's Day.

- When ordering several bouquets, corsages and boutonnieres, the florist should be willing to provide a free “toss” bouquet for the bride.

- Consider having your bouquets and arrangements done by the floral department at a local supermarket. Their prices are usually lower than a regular florist. You’ll need to designate someone to pick them up on the day of the wedding, but the savings could be well worth the effort.

- Use the bridesmaids’ bouquets to decorate the cake table and guest book table instead of ordering extra flowers.

- Assign someone the task of moving the altar bouquets from the ceremony to the reception site.

- Many florists will provide the groom’s boutonniere for free when you are ordering a group of boutonnieres.

- Purchase inexpensive pew bows (or make your own) to decorate the pews instead of using floral arrangements. Place a bow on every other row instead of each one. It will save you half the cost.

- Instead of a bouquet of flowers, choose a single, impressive bloom, like a lily or orchid, for you and your bridesmaids to carry.

- Use flowering potted plants as centerpieces on guest tables at your reception. You can find inexpensive ones at home improvement centers and discount stores. After the reception, give them away as gifts to your wedding helpers.

Fun Ideas:

- Instead of a traditional headpiece, wear a floral wreath (with or without a veil). Your bridesmaids can wear floral wreath headpieces, as well.

- Make small corsages or boutonnieres (real or silk) for each guest at your wedding. Present them as they arrive at the ceremony. Make extras in case you have more guests than anticipated. This is a fun way to express how much you appreciate their attendance at your special event.

- Consider adding a few orange blossoms to the flowers in your bouquet, as brides have done for centuries. The orange tree bears flowers and fruit simultaneously, a trait which symbolizes abundance and fulfillment. Carrying blossoms from the orange tree in the wedding bouquet was thought to bestow the blessing of happiness and nurturing on the new marriage.

Pitfall #12: Let's Be Candid

Photographs and videos are an important reminder of your special event, so choose these vendors carefully. Interview several photographers and/or videographers and check samples of their work before making your decision. These people will be in your face (literally) for hours, so you want to feel comfortable with them.

Ask them if they are familiar with your ceremony and reception sites, as well as what photography restrictions may apply. Also, find out how they will be dressed at the wedding.

Make sure the photographer is capable of taking candid shots at the reception. A wedding is not a photo shoot. You want to spend time with your guests at the reception—not posing for the photographer. Posed shots should be taken before the wedding and for no longer than twenty to thirty minutes after the ceremony.

Keep your photographer's and/or videographer's names and phone numbers in your wedding binder, as well as your contracts and receipts.

Helpful Hints:

- Provide the photographer and/or videographer with a copy of your wedding party list. This will help them with the group shots before the wedding, as well as candid shots at the reception.

- Assign someone to point out important family members and friends to the photographer and videographer.

- To guarantee you'll get the photos you want from your wedding ceremony and reception, give your photographer a list of essential subjects beforehand, such as an invitation close-up, favors on tables, bride and bridesmaids' bouquets and table centerpiece close-ups.

- To look slimmer in your wedding photos, turn slightly to one side, for a 3/4 view, rather than facing forward. And don't forget your posture—stand up straight and tall!

Money Saving Tips:

- Hire the photographer and/or videographer for the ceremony only, and have family members or friends take candid shots or videos at the reception.

- If your photography budget is extremely limited, hire a photography student from a local college.

Fun Ideas:

- Place disposable cameras on the guest tables at the reception, along with a note encouraging guests to take candid shots during the event. Assign an assistant to collect the cameras and drop them off at a pre-determined site to have the pictures developed.

- Another option is to place one-time-use video recorders on a few tables so guests can record their favorite party moments and special messages to you and the groom. Or have several friends and family members bring their own video cameras to cover the action during the reception.

- Ask a friend to take Polaroid pictures of each guest or guest couples as they arrive at the reception. The assistant can place the photos in an album and have the guests write personal messages to you and the groom next to their pictures. You'll have an instant scrapbook of your reception.

- If the weather isn't exactly perfect, make it the backdrop for some of your photos, such as stormy skies behind a portrait of you and the groom or candid shots of your groomsmen having a snowball fight.

- Offer the guests at your reception a fun glimpse into your past by creating a slideshow of pictures of you and your groom, set to music. You can include childhood shots, as well as photos of your courtship, engagement and wedding planning, parties and other wedding events.

- For extra entertainment, set up a television monitor during the last hour of the reception and play the video footage that your videographer (professional or amateur) has shot during the earlier part of the event.

- Ask your photographer to take post-reception shots, such as rose petals scattered on the grass after you and the groom have departed, your mother packing up gifts or floral arrangements or even the janitor sweeping the dance floor.

- Have a friend take digital photos of your wedding ceremony and reception so that you and the groom can view them on the way to your honeymoon.

Pitfall #13: The Sounds of Music

Music plays a very important role at both your wedding ceremony and your reception, setting the tone for your event. You and the groom will need to decide what type of music you want during your ceremony. The possibilities can include a pianist, organist, string quartet, guitarist, flutist, harpist, choir, vocalist or any number of combinations of the above.

For your reception, the choices are equally varied, including: a Disk Jockey (D.J.), pianist, string quartet, or a wide range of band musicians from "big band era" to swing to rock.

Your musician choices will be determined, not only by your personal taste in music, but by your budget priorities. These decisions might take some negotiation between you and the groom, so allow plenty of time and patience for this category.

If your wedding will be held at a church, be sure to check with the clergy regarding any restrictions involving music selections. Also, make sure the ceremony site you choose can accommodate your music vision.

Do you want the rafters to vibrate with the sounds of a pipe organ and the church doesn't own one?

Do you want a simple string quartet, but the church is a cavernous cathedral that will swallow up the delicate strains of the instruments? Plan your ceremony music to fit the ceremony site or vice versa.

The same considerations apply to the site you choose for your reception. If you want a large band and a dance floor that can accommodate a large crowd, keep this in mind when deciding on your reception venue.

When shopping for musicians, try to attend one of their performances, if possible, before you decide to hire them. Check their references and get referrals from friends. Make sure that the musicians you choose are reliable, professional (both in behavior and attire) and prompt.

If you decide to use a band for your reception music, make sure they are capable of performing songs from a wide range of music genres to accommodate all your guests.

After choosing your musicians, you'll need to meet with them to select the specific songs that are to be played during various parts of the ceremony and reception.

Keep the musicians' names and phone numbers in your wedding binder, along with your contracts and receipts.

Helpful Hint:

- If you want your musician or D.J. to act as the master of ceremonies during the reception, make sure he has a complete timeline for the evening, so he can announce the events, such as the first dance, toasts, cake cutting and bouquet and garter toss.

Money Saving Tips:

- Costs for musicians vary widely. A D.J. at the reception is much less expensive than a band, and can provide a much wider variety of music to accommodate guests of all ages.

- If you have a friend or relative who is outgoing and musically inclined, ask him or her to play CD's and make the necessary announcements during your reception.

- If you prefer to have a band play at your reception, but can't afford to have them play for more than just a few hours, bring in a D.J. for the later part of the evening so you can keep dancing on into the night without breaking the bank.

Fun Ideas:

- You and the groom can learn a special dance (such as the tango) to perform for your first dance together at the reception.

- Surprise your parents, in-laws and the married members of your wedding party by playing the first-dance songs from their weddings after your own first dance. Be sure to announce the songs and their significance.

- A great way to make sure all your guests' music favorites are covered is to ask them to write down a few selections on their RSVP cards. Then compile a list for your band or D.J.

- For a unique idea for your ceremony music, consider hiring an acoustical guitar player instead of a pianist or string quartet.

- If the theme for your wedding is the Renaissance period, hire a harpsichord player to set the perfect tone for your ceremony.

- If the weather is less than perfect, make light of the situation by asking your D.J. to play tunes like: "Raindrops Keep Falling on my Head" for a rainy day, "Heat Wave" if the temperature is balmy or "Let It Snow" during a blizzard.

- If you're planning a beach theme wedding, whether it's actually on the beach or staged indoors, hire a calypso band to set the perfect tone.

- Hire professional dancers or dance instructors to encourage your guests to get out onto the dance floor. A few possibilities: waltz, salsa, tango, country-western or belly-dancing.

Pitfall #14: A Bride Without a Ride

Hiring special transportation for the bride and groom can add a special touch to an important event. The options are endless and can be quite fun. Prices vary widely, of course, but if you get creative, you can usually find a solution to fit even a meager wedding budget.

Most couples choose a limousine to transport them from the church to the reception, then on to the honeymoon hotel. However, for a weekend limousine rental, there is usually a minimum four-hour charge.

Be sure to compare costs with several vendors for hourly rates and minimum charges. Also, check requirements for deposits, as well as cancellation policies.

As with any wedding vendor, check references and get referrals—you don't want to have to hitch a ride to the reception with one of your guests.

Keep the vendor's name and phone number in your wedding binder, as well as your contract and receipt.

Money Saving Tips:

- Instead of a limousine, rent a luxury car (a white Cadillac or Continental) for the day, and have one of your groomsmen drive you to the reception and your honeymoon hotel or airport.

- If your reception is held at a hotel, stay in the honeymoon suite at the same hotel and take the elevator up to your room—no extra transportation required. Many hotels give a discount on the room if the reception is held there.

Fun Ideas:

- If you are having a theme wedding, you might consider renting a vintage car, a horse drawn carriage, a boat, etc. to match your theme.

- Make a really grand exit from your reception by zipping off in a motorboat, taking off in a helicopter or floating away in a hot air balloon.

Pitfall #15: It's All in the Details

Now that you have decided on most of the big ticket items for your wedding, you need to purchase all those nit-picky little details we usually lump under the category of wedding accessories. These include items such as the garter, unity candle, guest book, ring bearer pillow, flower girl basket, champagne glasses, cake knife, wedding bubbles or birdseed bags, gifts for the wedding party, party favors for guests, etc.

Individually, these items don't cost a lot, but lumped together, they can take a sizeable bite out of the wedding budget. It's a good idea to make a list of everything you think you'll need and do some window shopping just to get a feel for what these items will cost. You can find most of them at wedding supply stores, gift stores and craft stores or by mail through catalogs or the internet.

An additional cost that falls into this category is decorations for the ceremony and reception. These can range widely from simple pew bows at the church to elaborate table centerpieces on each guest table at the reception. Setting priorities for the decorating budget in advance, based on the vision you have for your wedding, will help you avoid a budget-busting pitfall.

When it's time to do your final budget for wedding accessories and decorations, make a list of all the items you want for your ceremony and reception and assign each one a dollar amount. Check off the items as they are purchased and write down the actual amount spent to make sure you are staying on track with your budget.

This list will also come in handy when it's time to gather all the items to take with you on the day of the wedding. You don't want to leave any serious gaps in your wedding ceremony because the unity candle or ring bearer's pillow was left behind on the dining room table.

Keep all your receipts and/or mail orders for these purchases in your wedding binder in case you need to return or exchange some of them at the last minute.

Money Saving Tips:

- Make your own pew bows, table centerpieces for the reception, party favors for guests or birdseed bags. This can be a fun family or bridesmaids' group effort. There are a variety of idea books and supplies available at craft stores.

- Take advantage of reception facilities that might already be decorated for holidays, such as Christmas, to save on decorating costs.

- For a tropical themed wedding reception, ask friends and family to lend any large potted plants they might own to help decorate your facility. For extra sparkle, decorate them with tiny twinkle lights.

- For a garden themed wedding, ask for donations of arbors and benches, which you can decorate with tulle and twinkle lights. Also ask for any flowering, potted plants for an extra touch of color.

- If your budget is limited, skip the chintzy favors that most guests will toss in the trash. Instead, opt for something small but decadent, like a single piece of gourmet chocolate elegantly wrapped.

- If you or a family member likes to bake, whip up a batch of your favorite homemade cookies. Make them ahead of time and keep them in the freezer. If properly stored, they can be frozen for up to two months. Thaw and allow the cookies to come to room temperature before packaging them in clear, cellophane bags tied with a pretty ribbon.

Fun Ideas:

- Instead of birdseed bags or wedding bubbles, have your guests throw colorful paper streamers or rose petals at you and the groom while departing the reception.

- Give your guests tiny silver bells to ring when you and the groom leave the reception. The bells can serve double duty as favors for your guests to keep.

- For a fall wedding, crumble the leaves of fall foliage to make confetti for your guests to toss at you and the groom as you leave the reception. It's free and quite festive. You can bundle them in tulle circles tied with ribbon, like birdseed bags.

- Instead of having a traditional guest book, provide an album filled with photos of you and the groom with space on each page for guests to sign. It will encourage them to be more spontaneous and create fond memories for your special day.

- You can also have your guests sign the mat around a framed photo of you and the groom. Be sure the mat is extra-wide to give your guests plenty of room to express their best wishes.

- Use "floriography" (the language of flowers and herbs) to make wedding potpourri. Create a blend of herbs or flowers to express your feelings, such as: lavender for devotion, marjoram for joy, chamomile for patience, rosemary for remembrance, sage for wisdom and rosebuds for love.

  Give each guest a small bag of the potpourri to toss when you and the groom leave the reception. You can attach a tag to each bag that says: "This wedding potpourri contains lavender for devotion, marjoram for joy, etc."

  A few more floriography meanings are listed below:

Allspice	Compassion
Basil	Good Wishes
Caraway	Faithfulness
Chervil	Sincerity
Daisy	Innocence
Thyme	Happiness
Violet	Faith

- Personalize your wedding favors and let them do double duty as place cards on your guest tables. They will also serve as decorations. A few examples are listed below:

    - Sugar cookies with the guests names written in icing, bagged in clear cellophane bags and tied with ribbon. These can be cut out into any shape using cookie cutters to match your wedding theme.

    - Small decorative picture frames with the guests names printed on a card and inserted in the frame. Your guests can use them at home for displaying their own photographs.

    - Ball-shaped glass Christmas ornaments on which the guests' names are written with a gold or silver paint pen. Buy them after Christmas when they are on sale. Choose colors that match your wedding theme. Nestle each ornament in a candle wreath made of artificial greenery. These make beautiful decorations for your guest tables, and you can use them during any season—not just Christmas.

      Clear glass balls are especially pretty to use for a Winter Wonderland theme. Fill each one with a bit of artificial snow and silver glitter. Write the guests names on each one using a silver paint pen. Place the ornament in a glittery silver candle wreath.

- Make your own party crackers. Cut a 5” square of poster board, roll it into a tube, overlapping the ends 1/4” and tape together. Wrap it with colorful wrapping paper with the ends extending at least 3” beyond the tube on each end. Gather the wrapping paper close to one end of the tube and tie with ribbon to secure.

  Fill the tube with a few individually wrapped pieces of candy then gather the wrapping paper at the open end and tie with ribbon. Write the guests’ names on the crackers using a paint pen and place them on the guest tables.

Creative Ideas for Theme Weddings

No one wants a "cookie-cutter wedding". By choosing a theme that has personal meaning to you, your wedding will be unique. It is also easier to plan an event when you have a theme.

When you're ready to start planning, make a list of any ideas that have to do with your theme: colors, food, people, clothing styles, music, books, costumes, locations or historical facts. You might need to do a bit of research for historical periods but it will make your theme more authentic. This list will help you choose the invitations, wedding attire, decorations, food and music for your event.

Use the following suggestions to spark your creativity for planning a theme wedding:

- A time era:
    - The Renaissance period: Print your invitations on parchment paper and roll them up like scrolls and tie with ribbon. Choose Renaissance style dresses made from velvet or brocade fabric for your wedding gown and attendants' dresses. Incorporate music played on a harpsichord.

- The Victorian era: Include lots of lace, hearts, pearls, fans and satin ribbons on everything from invitations to bouquets. The bride and attendants can wear high-necked Victorian-style gowns and carry lace fans embellished with roses, ribbons and pearls. The men can wear top hats for a formal wedding.

- The Roaring 20's: Use slinky fabrics with lots of fringe for your wedding gown and attendants dresses. Wear long strands of beads and headbands with feathers. The men can wear 1920's style "zoot suits" or formal tails.

- The love and peace 60's: This time period is best suited for a casual style wedding that is held in a scenic park. Wear loose, unstructured gowns in gauzy fabric. Attendants' dresses can be made from bright colors or even tie-dyed fabric. Wear floral headpieces and incorporate lots of flowers into your decorations.

- A location: A tropical island, the beach, Paris, Venice, a garden, the jungle, a Southern plantation, a theme park. Study the details of each location carefully to reproduce the sights, sounds, colors and ambiance of each location for your wedding.

- A flower: Roses, daisies, sunflowers, lavender, tulips, lilies or daffodils. Include your chosen flower on invitations, the fabrics for dresses, in bouquets and boutonnieres, table decorations, favors and wedding cake.

- A season: Winter Wonderland, Summer Magic, "Fall"-ing in Love or Love "Springs" Eternal. Make a list of everything you can think of that has to do with the season you want to use for your theme. Then saturate your wedding with the sights, scents, tastes and colors that represent that particular season.

- An object: Butterflies, doves, swans, wreaths, candles, celestial/stars, hearts, wedding bells, Victoria fans or wedding rings. Whatever object you choose, incorporate it into everything from the invitations to the decorations to clothing to food.

- A holiday or celebration:
  - Christmas
  - Mardi Gras
  - Valentine's Day
  - Fourth of July
  - New Year's Eve

- A color, such as black and white: the bride wears white, the men wear black tuxedos, the attendants wear black dresses trimmed in white and the flower girl wears white trimmed in black. Attendants can carry red, pink or yellow roses for a punch of color. Serve "tuxedo" strawberries dipped in white and dark chocolate. Cover guest tables with white tablecloths with black toppers. Centerpieces can be red, pink or yellow roses (real or silk) in sleek silver or glass bowls for a contemporary touch. The wedding cake can have narrow black bands of ribbon or icing around the base of each tier. Add a bouquet of red, pink or yellow roses on top.

- Books or movies: Gone with the Wind, The Great Gatsby, Treasure Island, Titanic or any movie or book with a theme that appeals to you. Watch the movie and pay particular attention to the details of clothing, hair styles, jewelry, decorations, music food and accessories so you can capture the same feel at your wedding.

- Miscellaneous themes:

    - Western
    - Country
    - Fairytale or Fantasy
    - Las Vegas/Casino
    - Nautical
    - Musical
    - Hawaiian Luau
    - Hollywood

Choose a theme that has special meaning for you and the groom. It will help make your wedding planning easier and the event more memorable for you and your guests.

Creative Ideas for Table Centerpieces

- Use flowering potted plants for spring and summer weddings or poinsettias for a Christmas wedding. You can find inexpensive ones at home improvement centers and discount stores. Give the plants away as gifts to your wedding helpers.

- For fall weddings, arrange small pumpkins, gourds, colorful fall leaves and dried ears of corn into creative centerpieces for your guest tables or serving tables.

- For a country themed wedding, use a small basket with a handle, lined with a blue and white checked napkin and filled with red apples for each guest table centerpiece. Use blue and white gingham fabric for tablecloths.

- For a simple, but elegant centerpiece for guest tables, use one white pillar candle on a small silver-colored tray, placed under an inexpensive glass hurricane shade. Surround the base with silk or real greenery. Use white tablecloths.

- For a garden themed wedding, use white wire birdcages (found at craft centers or import stores) topped with colorful silk flowers, tulle and ribbon. Tablecloths can be pretty pastel colors.

- For a winter wonderland theme, use white table cloths, and place three white pillar candles of staggered heights on a square mirror. Sprinkle silver wrapped chocolates (kisses) around the table top. You can also sprinkle silver glitter or confetti on the table top if allowed at your site.

- Float candles in a clear, round fish bowl. You can tint the water with food coloring to match your wedding theme colors if you like. Sprinkle a coordinating color of glitter or confetti around the bowl, if allowed.

- For a beach theme, fill tall hurricane vases with water and goldfish. Surround the bases with sand and seashells. Incorporate lots of aqua and teal into your decorating scheme to evoke a feeling of the ocean.

- Make a fun and edible flower cookie centerpiece. Cut out flower shapes from sugar cookie dough and bake them with a wooden skewer inserted in one end. Ice with colorful frosting, let dry and cover each with a clear cellophane bag, tied with ribbon. Insert each cookie flower into a brightly painted terracotta pot filled with florist's foam which is covered with paper shred. Each cookie is also a wedding favor for guests.

- For a Mardi Gras theme, use metallic green or purple masks for place cards, writing the guests' names on them with a gold paint pen. Use purple and green pillar candles on a mirror square for the centerpiece. Sprinkle purple, green and gold Mardi Gras beads around the table top.

- Decorate cupcakes and stack them on tiered serving plates for your centerpieces instead of having one big wedding cake. Make all the cupcakes ahead of time and freeze them. Decorate the day before the wedding to match your theme.

- For a Victorian wedding start collecting teapots at garage sales and flea markets or borrow them from friends and family. They make beautiful centerpieces when filled with real or silk greenery or flowers. You can also find inexpensive china cups and saucer sets at garage sales and flea markets to give away as favors. Put a tea light inside and place one for each guest on the tables.

Creative Ideas for Guest Favors

It's fun to make your own guest favors that match the theme of your wedding. There are hundreds of how-to books at craft stores to give you ideas. Gather your friends and family and make it a group activity.

If you're pressed for time or just aren't crafty, check out the creative ideas for favors offered by hundreds of companies on the internet. You can find favors to fit your theme on any budget.

Below is a list of favor possibilities you can make yourself:

- For a garden theme, buy small herb plants and transfer them to tiny terra cotta pots. Include a tag with instructions for care and attach with a ribbon tied around the pot. You can paint the pots to match your wedding colors and even print the guests' names on them to use as place cards.

- For a Winter Wonderland theme, make divinity candy or meringue cookies for your favors. Wrap one or two in plastic then place on a white tulle circle. Gather up the edges of the circle and tie with a silver ribbon. For the divinity, add a small tag that says, "Love is divine".

- For a beach or tropical theme, make candles in small sea shells. Melt candle wax (any color), pour it into the shell and add a wick. You can find the supplies and instructions at most craft stores. Use them as table decorations, as well as guest favors.

- Make your own party crackers. Cut a 5” square of poster board, roll it into a tube, overlapping the ends 1/4” and tape together). Wrap it with colorful wrapping paper with the ends extending at least 3” beyond the tube on each end. Gather the wrapping paper close to one end of the tube and tie with ribbon to secure. Fill the tube with a few individually wrapped pieces of candy then gather the wrapping paper at the open end and tie with ribbon. You can also write your guests names on the favors so they can double as place cards.

- Wrap candy or coated nuts in colorful tulle circles to make easy and inexpensive favors that can also decorate your guest tables. Cut 8” circles from tulle or purchase circles that are already cut and place the candy or nuts in the center. Gather up the tulle and tie with a pretty ribbon. You can also use two circles of different colored tulle.

- Use candy molds and melted white chocolate, which can be tinted any color, or different colors of brown chocolate, to make candy in shapes to match your theme: roses, sea shells, snowflakes, butterflies, etc. Place the candy in clear cellophane bags and tie with ribbon.

- Small flower arrangements at each place setting can double as wedding favors and table decorations. Buy tiny, inexpensive vases and use one or two blooms in each vase.

- Make clear cones from acetate paper that you can buy in the gift-wrap section of craft stores or discount stores. Simply cut an 8" square of acetate, roll it into a cone shape and secure with transparent tape. Place individually wrapped chocolates or hard candy inside. Gather the top and tie with ribbon to close. Trim the top edges off evenly. You can also line the cone with a silver or gold metallic paper doily. Cut an 8" doily into 4 pie-shaped wedges. Place the cut doily right side down on the acetate square. Align the square corner of the cut doily with the square edge of the acetate square and roll them up together. Tape closed at the back, insert the candy and tie with ribbon.

- There are lots of pretty wedding favor boxes available at your local craft or discount store in the wedding department that are inexpensive. You can also order them online. Fill the boxes with the candy of your choice, such as individually wrapped chocolates or candy-coated almonds.

Pitfall #16: By the Light of the Moon

An extended honeymoon to an exotic location is a luxury that most couples can't afford, but the price and destination options for honeymoon possibilities can vary so widely that even couples on a limited budget can find a creative solution.

Just one night in a luxurious, near-by hotel might be the perfect ending for your wedding day. Once again, your wedding budget priorities will determine the type of honeymoon you can afford.

Whether your honeymoon is one night or two weeks, make sure you're dealing with a reputable company for all travel and hotel accommodations, especially for package deals. Glossy brochures can be misleading. If a deal sounds too good to be true, it probably is. Check out the travel company's references and complaint history with the Better Business Bureau.

Before choosing a honeymoon location, sight unseen, talk to people who've been to the area where you want to go. Find out what the hotel accommodations are like. Which restaurants are best? What local attractions are must see's or do's? Gather as much information as you can before making your decision.

Whether you are purchasing a package deal or buying airplane tickets and making hotel reservations separately, get all the details in writing, including confirmation numbers and contact information. Double-check the dates and be sure you understand the cancellation policies before handing over your money.

Travel insurance is always a wise investment when you are spending a considerable amount on the honeymoon—life has a way of throwing us little surprises when we least expect them. Once again, make sure that you're dealing with a reputable company and that you understand the conditions that are covered in your insurance policy.

If you're planning to honeymoon in a tropical location or on board a cruise ship traveling to a tropical destination, be sure to keep Mother Nature in mind. Don't schedule your honeymoon during hurricane or monsoon season. You might find your plans cancelled, or worse, you could be stranded under very unpleasant conditions.

Make sure the honeymoon you choose is within your wedding budget range before making your reservations. Keep all receipts and vendor information in your wedding binder.

Helpful Hints:

- If you plan to travel outside the U.S. for your honeymoon, you'll need a passport for most destinations. If you don't already have a passport, you can get an application online. It takes 4-6 weeks to process your application, unless you want to pay a stiff fee for faster service, so allow plenty of time to receive it.

- It's a good idea for you and the groom to make two copies of your passport, driver's license and birth certificates when traveling outside the U.S. Leave one copy at home, and keep one in your suitcase in a separate place than where you are storing your original documents.

- If you plan to fly to your honeymoon destination, pack part of your clothes in your husband's suitcase and part of his clothes in yours. If one of your bags is lost, you'll both have clothes to wear while waiting for the return of your luggage.

- Pack really important items, such as currency, medications, hotel confirmation, passports and plane tickets, plus one change of clothes in your carry-on bag, so you'll be covered in case your luggage is lost.

- If you plan to do much shopping while on your honeymoon, pack an empty tote bag in your suitcase to carry souvenirs home.

Money Saving Tips:

- If your reception is held at an elegant hotel, stay in the honeymoon suite at the same hotel for your honeymoon. Many hotels give a discount on the room if the reception is held there.

- Staying at an all-inclusive resort, such as Sandals or Couples, can save money on your honeymoon budget. They usually include lots of extras in their room rates, from meals and alcoholic beverages to activities and live entertainment.

- Buying a vacation package instead of booking your airfare, hotel accommodations and rental car separately can save money.

- Choose your honeymoon location based on off-season rates. In fall, save money on discounted rates on Hawaii hotel rooms; in summer, head to the Caribbean or Mexico to save on "low-season" rates. Check with your travel agent to find other discounts and plan your wedding date accordingly.

Fun Ideas:

- Keep a daily journal during your honeymoon. Record special events, feelings, humorous accounts and memorable interactions with your new husband. You will enjoy reliving these memories years later, especially on your wedding anniversaries.

- If the honeymoon is highest on your budget priority list, consider having a "destination" wedding. A small group of friends and family fly with the bride and groom to a unique destination for a weekend wedding event. Then the guests depart and the bride and groom stay for the honeymoon. If you hold your destination wedding at a full-service resort, the staff will help you plan the event and book everything you need. Now that's a stress-free wedding!

Other Helpful Hints to Avoid Wedding Pitfalls

- Consider getting event insurance if you are spending a large amount of money on your wedding. You can find information about these companies on the internet or in bridal magazines. Once again, check references and make sure you're dealing with a reputable company.

- Make sure you are aware of the cancellation or refund policies for all your wedding vendors before you sign a contract. Read the "fine print" on all contracts and make sure you understand what you are signing.

- Pay your vendors using a credit card instead of cash or check whenever possible. You can contest the charges with the credit card company and get your money refunded if your vendor doesn't deliver what he/she promised.

- Make sure you are up to date on any partial payments you're scheduled to make, such as those to the caterer or baker. Having your food and cake held hostage at the last minute can really spoil the fun.

- One week before the wedding, call all your vendors and ceremony and reception sites to confirm the dates, times and details of your orders and reservations. This task should be a snap since you've kept everything neatly filed in your handy wedding binder.

- Designate someone ahead of time to transport any gifts that may arrive at the wedding reception to your home, so your mother isn't burdened with this task. Wedding gifts should be delivered to the bride's home, or other designated address, before the wedding.

- Don't schedule the bachelor or bachelorette party the night before the wedding. You want to be looking and feeling your best for this very important day. You're about to make a lifetime commitment, so you need to be alert.

On the Day of the Wedding

At last! You've finished all the planning and coordinating, and negotiating and budgeting. You still have your sanity and the groom hasn't bolted for the door yet. Hallelujah!

The most important thing to remember on your wedding day is to relax, slow down and enjoy every moment of it. The hours in this day will fly by like minutes, so make sure you don't miss any of the joy they hold for you. You've done everything you can to prepare up to this point, so consider the following suggestions and let the fun begin.

- Don't get so busy on the day of the wedding that you forget to eat. You don't want to faint at the altar from too much stress, combined with a low blood sugar level. A light meal shortly before you head for the ceremony is a good plan, especially since you might not have time to eat during the reception.

- Ask for help. Not everyone can afford the services of a wedding consultant, but that doesn't mean you have to handle all the wedding day tasks yourself. You want to enjoy yourself on this special day, so recruit assistants for decorating, distributing flowers, setting up the buffet, serving cake and beverages, manning the guest book, announcing reception events, etc. Delegate!

- When choosing a hairstyle for your wedding day, don't go overboard with an outrageous "do" that makes you feel self-conscious. The same rule applies for your make-up. You want to look natural and feel like yourself.

- Take an emergency kit with you to your wedding. Include extra panty hose, antacids, headache medicine and sewing kit (a needle, scissors and white and black thread for last minute repairs). Also helpful are bobby pins, safety pins, rubber bands, band-aids, hair spray, comb and brush.

- Try to relax and enjoy your wedding. Don't morph into the dreaded "bridezilla" if things don't go exactly as planned. You'll want to take fond memories of this day into your marriage. A wedding is, after all, just a very short ceremony followed by a great big party.

Fun Ideas:

- After the wedding and honeymoon, choose your favorite photos from both events and create a website for friends and family. Add captions describing where you were, what you were doing and what you were feeling at the time.

- After you return from your honeymoon, host a party for all your attendants to thank them for participating in your wedding. Share honeymoon photos and present souvenir gifts from your honeymoon location.

- Need a really special gift for your groom that doesn't cost a bundle? You can have a star named after your sweetheart as a wedding gift to him. The International Star Registry has been naming stars for celebrities and dignitaries worldwide for years. The gift package includes a parchment certificate, available framed or unframed, with the name of the person you are naming a star after, the dedication date, and telescopic coordinates of the star. You'll also receive a booklet with charts of the constellations plus a larger, more detailed chart with the star you've named circled in red. These star names are copyrighted with their telescopic coordinates in the book, *Your Place in the Cosmos*, so future generations can identify the star name in the directory and, using a telescope, locate the actual star in the sky. It is the gift of a lifetime. Contact them online at: www.starregistry.com.

A Really Fun Idea:

- If you and the groom decide that you don't want the hassles of planning a large wedding, but you still want your family and close friends to attend, have a surprise wedding.

  Invite your guests to a regular party and surprise them with a wedding. Then you'll have lots of extra money to spend on your honeymoon, or maybe use for a down payment on your first house!

Index

About the Author

Gloria Hander Lyons has channeled 30 years of training and hands-on experience in the areas of art, interior decorating, crafting and event planning into writing creative how-to books.

Her books cover a wide range of topics including decorating your home, cooking, planning weddings and tea parties, crafting and self publishing.

She has designed original needlework and craft projects featured in magazines, including *Better Homes and Gardens, McCall's, Country Handcrafts* and *Crafts*.

Gloria also teaches interior decorating, self publishing and wedding planning classes at her local community college and offers private classes and workshops.

Much to her family's delight, her kitchen is in non-stop test mode, creating recipes for new cookbooks.

Check out her monthly newsletter for free craft ideas, decorating and event planning tips and taste-tempting recipes at **www.BlueSagePress.com**.

Other Books by Gloria Hander Lyons

- *Easy Microwave Desserts in a Mug*
- *Easy Microwave Desserts in a Mug for Kids*
- *No Rules – Just Fun Decorating*
- *Just Fun Decorating for Tweens & Teens*
- *Decorating Basics: For Men Only!*
- *If Teapots Could Talk: Fun Ideas for Tea Parties*
- *Hand Over the Chocolate and No One Gets Hurt! A Chocolate-Lover's Cookbook*
- *Designs That Sell: How To Make Your Home Show Better and Sell Faster*
- *A Taste of Lavender: Delectable Treats with an Exotic Floral Flavor*
- *Lavender Sensations: Fragrant Herbs for Home & Bath*
- *Self-Publishing on a Budget: A Do-It-All-Yourself Guide*
- *The Secret Ingredient: Tasty Recipes with an Unusual Twist*

Blue Sage Press Booklets & Doll Patterns

We publish a series of booklets, ranging from 24 to 36 pages, on a wide variety of topics, plus fabric doll patterns. Visit our website or write for a complete list.

A sample of our booklet titles:

- *Flamingoes, Poodle Skirts & Red Hots: Creative Theme Party Ideas*
- *Conquer the Clutter: Simple Steps for De-Cluttering Your Home*
- *Teapots & Teddy Bears: Fun Children's Tea Parties*
- *Gifts in a Jar: Brownies, Cookies & Cakes*
- *Gifts in a Jar: Muffins, Breads & Scones*
- *Don't Eat the Biscuits: Easy Biscuit Quilting Projects*
- *It's Just Paint! Decorative Painting For Furniture, Fabrics & Walls*
- *Ten Common Home Decorating Mistakes & How to Avoid Them*
- *Your Favorite Meals in a Muffin*

A sample of our fabric doll patterns:

- *Welcome Angel: 16" Hanging Angel holds a heart garland that says "Welcome"*
- *You're Sew Special: 14" Shelf-sitter Angel holds sewing supplies and a heart sign that says "You're Sew Special"*
- *Teachers Are Beary Special: 16" Hanging Bear holds a heart garland that says "Teachers Are Beary Special"*
- *Apples For Emily: 14" Piggy holds a basket of apples and sign that says "Apples 5¢"*
- *Nurses Call the Shots: 14" Shelf-sitter Nurse doll holds her chart & thermometer*
- *Wash Day for Sadie: 18" Mammie doll with her basket of laundry*
- *Hand Over the Chocolate: 14" Shelf-sitter kitty bandit holds her rolling pin and sign: "Hand Over the Chocolate"*

Ordering Information

To order additional copies of this book, send check or money order payable to:

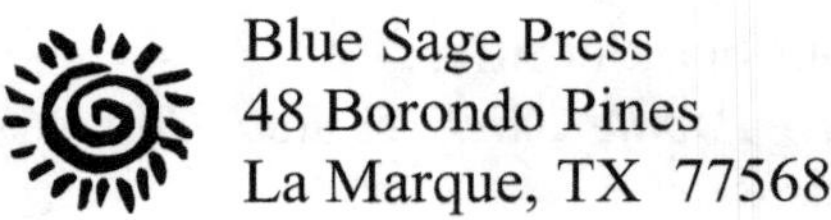

Cost for this edition is $7.95 per book (U.S. currency only) plus $3.50 shipping and handling for the first book and $1.50 for each additional book shipped to the same U.S. address.

Texas residents add 8.25% sales tax to total order amount.

To pay by credit card or get a complete list of books, booklets and doll patterns by Gloria Hander Lyons, visit our website:

www.BlueSagePress.com

www.ingramcontent.com/pod-product-compliance
Lightning Source LLC
LaVergne TN
LVHW020650100826
845148LV00012B/2418

* 9 7 8 0 9 7 9 0 6 1 8 4 4 *